Fun Fan Facts:
The Unofficial NBA Edition

Cleveland Cavaliers

Everything Young Cavaliers
Fans Should Know

By: Jake Liam

Dedication

To every Cavaliers fan who stayed through the bad seasons, the heartbreaks, and the "maybe next year" moments. The 2016 championship was for all of you.

THE NBA BY THE NUMBERS

MOST NBA CHAMPIONSHIPS*

- CELTICS (18) †
- LAKERS (17)
- WARRIORS (7)
- BULLS (6)
- SPURS (5)

As of the 2024-25 Season. † One Trophy = 4 Championships.

NBA HISTORY SNAPSHOT

- **1946** NBA Founded
- **1954** Shot Clock Introduced
- **1979** 3-Point Line Added
- **2023** NBA Cup Introduced

BIG NUMBERS

$156 million
Stephen Curry's est. earnings in the 24-25 season

7'7"
Tallest player in NBA history (Gheorghe Mureşan & Manute Bol)

---

30 Teams Competing in the NBA

4 Playoff Rounds

82 Games Per Season

CLEVELAND CAVALIERS
IN THE NBA

- FOUNDED: 1970 †
- NBA TITLES: 1
- CONFERENCE TITLES: 5*

42 Playoff Appearances

*† Founding dates are complicated & may cause arguments at Thanksgiving. Ask someone born before color TV. All Titles reflect pre-relocation franchise history. * As of 2024-25 Season.*

NBA ALL-TIME MVP LEADERS

KAREEM ABDUL-JABBAR (6) ★ MICHAEL JORDAN (5) ★ BILL RUSSELL (5)

EASTERN CONFERENCE

- Atlantic – **Celtics**
- Atlantic – **Nets**
- Atlantic – **Knicks**
- Atlantic – **76ers**
- Atlantic – **Raptors**
- Central – **Bulls**
- Central – **Cavaliers**
- Central – **Pistons**
- Central – **Pacers**
- Central – **Bucks**
- Southeast – **Hawks**
- Southeast – **Hornets**
- Southeast – **Heat**
- Southeast – **Magic**
- Southeast – **Wizards**

WESTERN CONFERENCE

- Pacific – **Lakers**
- Pacific – **Clippers**
- Pacific – **Warriors**
- Pacific – **Suns**
- Pacific – **Kings**
- Northwest – **Nuggets**
- Northwest – **Timberwolves**
- Northwest – **Thunder**
- Northwest – **Trail Blazers**
- Northwest – **Jazz**
- Southwest – **Mavericks**
- Southwest – **Rockets**
- Southwest – **Spurs**
- Southwest – **Pelicans**
- Southwest – **Grizzlies**

Introduction

Welcome, fans! Whether you're new to cheering for the Cleveland Cavaliers or you've been bleeding the team colors your whole life, this book is packed with fun, exciting facts about your favorite team. Get ready to impress your friends and family with everything you know about the Cavaliers.

Quick Time Out

This book is packed with stats. Like, A LOT of stats. Every fact was checked, double-checked, and triple-checked. But here's the thing about basketball history: not everyone agrees on everything. Ask someone who watched games before color TV and someone who grew up with instant replay and you'll get two completely different answers. My dad, stepdad, uncle, and grandpa all argued about the same fact. Four people. Four answers. All of them think they're right. So if you spot something that doesn't match what you've heard, congratulations. You might be a bigger fan than the people who helped make this book. And honestly? That's pretty cool.

HOW IT WORKS

THE SEASON
82 Games. One Goal.
Each team plays 82 games.
Win enough to make the
Playoffs.
Every game counts!

PLAYOFFS
30 Teams. 16 Make It.
8 per conference make the playoffs.
Win=Advance | Lose=Go Home
Best record
gets home court!

PLAYOFF ROUNDS
Best of 7. Win 4 or Go Home.
4 rounds of pure pressure.
Every series is do-or-die!

OVERTIME?
5 More Minutes.
Keep playing until
someone pulls ahead.
No ties. Ever.

THE FINALS
One Series. One Champion.
Winner lifts the Trophy.
Legend status unlocked.

How the NBA Works

At first glance, basketball feels simple. Ten players. One ball. Two hoops. Go.

Then the NBA adds the layers.

An 82-game regular season. A draft where bad teams pick first. Playoffs that last two full months. Superstars who can change everything with one trade. Dynasties that rise, fall, and rise again.

And somehow, it all works.

The NBA is built on one big idea: every team gets a chance to reset, reload, and rise again. No relegation. No dropping down to a lower league. Just basketball, every night, from October through June.

It is a league designed for drama, stars, and comebacks. And once you understand the flow, it is impossible to stop watching.

The League Setup

The NBA has 30 teams, spread across the United States and Canada. Those teams are split into two conferences:

- Eastern Conference
- Western Conference

Each conference has three divisions, mostly based on geography. Divisions matter for scheduling, but not as much as they used to.

Every team plays 82 regular season games, usually from October through April. Home games. Road games. Back-to-back nights. Long road trips. The season is a marathon before the sprint even starts.

Win games, and you climb the standings. Lose too many, and the pressure builds fast.

How Games Are Played

An NBA game has four quarters, each lasting 12 minutes. That means 48 minutes of game time, plus timeouts, free throws, and the occasional coach argument that adds another 20 minutes nobody planned for.

Scoring is simple:

- A shot inside the three-point line is worth 2 points
- A shot beyond the arc is worth 3 points
- Free throws are worth 1 point

If the score is tied at the end of regulation, the game goes to overtime, which lasts 5 minutes. Still tied? Another overtime. Keep going until someone wins.

There is a shot clock too. Teams have 24 seconds to take a shot. No standing around. No holding the ball forever. Keep it moving.

The Regular Season Race

The regular season is long for a reason. It tests everything.

Depth. Health. Focus. Patience.

Teams play opponents from both conferences, but they face conference rivals more often. By the end of the season, each conference's top teams have earned their playoff spots the hard way.

The goal is simple: make the playoffs. But there is a twist.

The NBA Cup

In 2023, the NBA added something new to the middle of the season. Something with actual stakes. They called it the In-Season Tournament, now known as the NBA Cup.

It works like this: Every team plays a small group stage during November and December, with special court designs that look like nothing else in basketball. The best teams advance to a knockout round held in Las Vegas.

The winners split a prize pool. Players earn bonus money. And for the first time, a team could lift a trophy before the playoffs even started.

Some fans are still warming up to it. Some players love it. But the moment a team starts treating it seriously and a crowd shows up buzzing in December, it feels like something.

Which, honestly, sounds about right.

The Play-In Tournament

Instead of sending the top eight teams from each conference straight to the playoffs, the NBA added something new. The Play-In Tournament.

Here is how it works:

- Teams ranked 1 through 6 in each conference are safe
- Teams ranked 7 through 10 fight for the final two playoff spots

The 7 and 8 seeds have an advantage. Win once and you are in. Lose and you still get one more shot. The 9 and 10 seeds have to win twice in a row just to earn a first-round matchup.

It turns the end of the season into a sprint. Every game suddenly matters more. Fans love it. Coaches age rapidly.

The NBA Playoffs

Once the playoffs begin, everything tightens.

Sixteen teams enter. Eight from each conference. Every round is a best-of-seven games series. That means the first team to win four games moves on:

- First Round
- Conference Semifinals
- Conference Finals
- NBA Finals

Home-court advantage matters. Crowds get louder. Rotations get shorter. Superstars play heavier minutes. One bad quarter can flip a series. One great performance can define a career.

By the time the NBA Finals arrive in June, only two teams are left. One from the East. One from the West. Four wins away from a championship. Four wins away from history.

The NBA Draft: Hope Begins Here

Here is where the NBA gets clever. Every summer, new players enter the league through the NBA Draft. Teams take turns selecting college players, international stars, and teenagers straight out of high school.

The teams that finished with the worst records get the best odds to pick early through the Draft Lottery. It is not guaranteed, but it gives struggling franchises a real shot at changing their future with one pick.

That means one bad season does not doom you forever. It might actually change everything. Some franchises are rebuilt by a single draft night moment. Hope shows up wearing a new jersey.

No Relegation. All Pressure.

Unlike many global sports leagues, NBA teams never drop down to a lower league. They always stay in the NBA.

That does not mean there is no pressure.

Fans remember losing seasons. Owners make changes. Coaches get replaced. Players get traded. Every year is a test of direction, patience, and belief.

Stars, Systems, and Showtime

The NBA is famous for its stars. But stars do not win alone.

Teams need chemistry. Coaches need systems. Role players need to deliver on the biggest stages. One injury. One hot streak. One trade deadline deal. Any of it can flip a season.

That balance between individual brilliance and team basketball is what makes the league special.

Fast breaks. Buzzer-beaters. Game 7s. And moments that get replayed forever. That is the NBA.

Once you get the flow, it is pure electricity.

Cleveland Cavaliers Facts

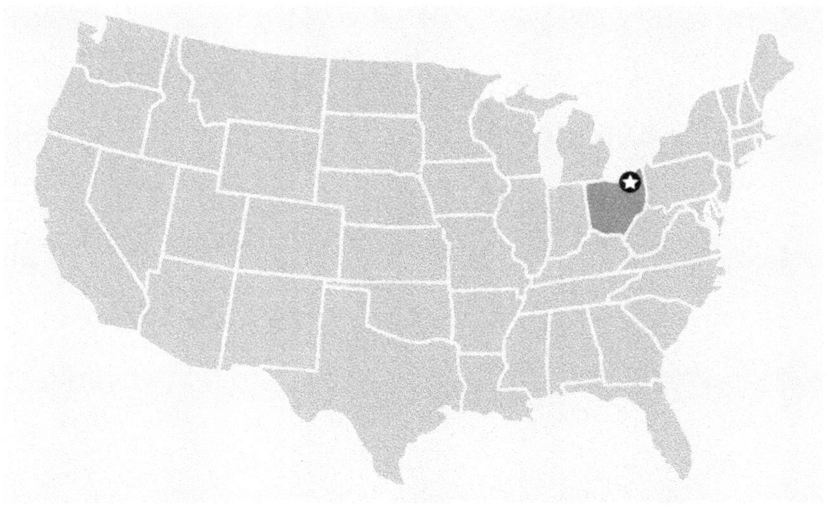

Home City

Cleveland, Ohio

Home City Metro Area Population

about 2 million

Home Arena

Rocket Arena

Max Capacity: 19,432

Famous Local Food

Pierogies, Polish Boy sandwiches, corned beef, Lake Erie perch

Conference / Division

Eastern / Central

Chapter 1: From the Rust Belt to the NBA

1. A City Gets a Team

In 1970, the NBA decided it was time to expand, and Cleveland, Ohio raised its hand. A local businessman named Nick Mileti put together a group of investors, convinced the league that Ohio was ready for professional basketball, and paid around $3.7 million for the privilege of building a team from absolute zero. No players. No history. No wins. Just a name, a logo, and enough optimism to fill an arena.

The name came from a fan contest won by a man named Jerry Tomko from Eastlake, Ohio, who submitted Cavaliers. Daring, bold, and unbothered by the odds. It was a perfect fit for a team that had no business being confident yet somehow was anyway. The first game on October 14, 1970 ended in a 110-99 loss to the San Diego Rockets, and the Cavaliers finished that debut season at 15-67, which is a polite way of saying they lost roughly four times for every time they won.

The fans still showed up. That is the thing about Cleveland that you need to understand before anything else in this book makes sense. Hand them a basketball team assembled from other teams' castoffs, give them a debut season that could charitably be described as educational, and they pack the building anyway. Cleveland was that kind of city from day one, and everything that came later only proved it more.

2. Wine and Gold: The Colors That Cleveland Made Famous

Before the Cavaliers played a single game, someone had to decide what the uniforms would look like, and they landed on wine, gold, and navy blue. Not red. Wine. Cleveland fans will correct you on this distinction immediately and with great enthusiasm, so it is worth locking in before you find yourself on the wrong end of that conversation.

The combination was bold, distinctive, and completely their own until the 1990s arrived and the franchise decided a rebrand was in order, switching to a murky palette of dark navy, black, and a bronze tone that nobody could quite agree on. It was a very 1990s decision, the kind that made perfect sense at the time and now sits in the historical record alongside other great choices of that era like wallet chains and Vanilla

Ice. Most Cavaliers fans have quietly agreed to skip over that chapter of the team's visual history entirely.

When the wine and gold returned in the early 2000s, the whole city exhaled. The colors felt right in a way the dark rebrand never had, like the team had been wearing someone else's jacket for a decade and finally found their own again. Nobody else in the NBA looks like Cleveland, and that is exactly the point.

3. The Miracle of Richfield

In 1974, the Cavaliers moved into a brand new arena called the Richfield Coliseum, and here is where the story gets genuinely strange. The Richfield Coliseum was not located in a city. Not near a city. Not even particularly close to a suburb. It sat on a stretch of open land between Cleveland and Akron, surrounded by farmland, in a township so rural that the arena basically had cows for neighbors. Someone approved a 20,000-seat professional basketball arena in the middle of the Ohio countryside and apparently nobody in the room thought to ask why.

Against all geographic logic, it worked beautifully. In 1976 the Cavaliers put together a magical playoff run, knocking out the defending champion Washington

Bullets in a Game 7 thriller on the way to the Eastern Conference Finals. Fans poured in from Cleveland, Akron, and every small town in between, drove through miles of dark Ohio farmland, and turned that impossible arena into one of the loudest buildings in basketball. The run earned a nickname that has stuck ever since: the Miracle of Richfield.

Then, two days before the Conference Finals against the Boston Celtics, starting center Jim Chones broke his foot in practice. Not in a game. Not in a collision. Practice. The Cavaliers lost the series without him and went home wondering what might have been, a question that would unfortunately become a recurring theme in Cleveland sports history.

4. The Shot

It is May 7, 1989, and the Cleveland Cavaliers are having their best season in franchise history with 57 wins, genuine playoff expectations, and a roster that finally looks like it belongs in a championship conversation. They face the Chicago Bulls in the first round, and through four games the series is tied at two apiece, everything riding on Game 5 in Cleveland.

With five seconds on the clock and the score tied, the Bulls inbound to Michael Jordan near halfcourt. Jordan comes off a screen, drifts sideways, and rises up over Cavaliers guard Craig Ehlo from just inside the free throw line. The ball drops through the net as the buzzer sounds, and Jordan launches into one of the most replayed celebrations in basketball history, jumping and pumping his fist while the arena falls completely silent around him. Ehlo sinks to the floor. Cleveland is done.

The moment became known simply as The Shot, which tells you everything about the size of the scar it left. Ehlo actually played decent defense on the play, which somehow makes it worse. Jordan was just in a different place that day, the kind of unstoppable that makes you feel less like you lost a game and more like you ran into a force of nature. Cleveland fans carried The Shot with them for years, and if you want a quick way to bring a very specific pain into a Cavaliers fan's eyes, all you have to do is mention Craig Ehlo's name.

5. The Owner Who Nearly Broke Everything

In 1980, a businessman named Ted Stepien bought the Cleveland Cavaliers and, within a remarkably short period of time, managed to threaten the long-term survival of the entire franchise through a combination of impulsive trades and a truly historic inability to leave well enough alone. In his first two seasons as owner he cycled through five head coaches, which works out to a new head coach roughly every five months, suggesting that either Stepien had extremely bad luck or extremely bad judgment, and the evidence strongly points toward the latter.

The real damage came from the trades. Stepien gave away future first-round draft picks so freely and so often that the Cavaliers burned through their ability to rebuild for years. Draft picks are the lifeblood of any team that is not winning right now, the seeds you plant so something can grow later, and Cleveland was handing them away like someone who plants a garden and then gives away all the seeds before anything can grow. The situation became so widely recognized as a disaster that the NBA created an official rule preventing any team from trading away first-round picks in consecutive years without retaining one for themselves. They named it the Stepien Rule, which is the kind of legacy most people would rather not leave behind.

The NBA helped engineer a sale to brothers Gordon and George Gund in 1983 specifically to remove Stepien from the equation, and the Cavaliers spent years carefully rebuilding what had been stripped away. They got there eventually. It just required patience, smart drafting, and a collective effort not to dwell too long on how unnecessary the whole detour had been.

Chapter 2: The Players Who Made Cleveland Proud

6. Austin Carr: The Original Cavalier ("Mr. Cavalier," 1971–1979)

Every franchise has a player who arrives before the building is even finished, before there is anything to inherit, and decides to become the foundation anyway. For Cleveland, that player was Austin Carr. A guard out of Notre Dame who had been one of the most prolific scorers in college basketball history, Carr was selected with the first overall pick in the 1971 draft, and the Cavaliers essentially handed him the keys to a franchise that had not figured out what it was yet and said good luck.

Carr spent his entire prime in Cleveland, playing with teams that were still figuring themselves out around him. He averaged over 20 points per game in his peak seasons, attacked the basket with a fearlessness that made opposing defenses uncomfortable, and became the first player in Cavaliers history that fans genuinely built an attachment to. He was not just a good player on a developing team. He was the reason to pay attention.

When people in Cleveland talk about the original Cavalier, they mean Carr without hesitation. He is the starting point of the entire story. Every great franchise needs its first icon, the one who shows up when there is nothing to show up for and makes himself impossible to ignore. Austin Carr was that for Cleveland, and the fans who watched him play have never forgotten it.

7. Mark Price: The Sharpshooter Nobody Saw Coming (1986–1995)

Mark Price was selected in the second round of the 1986 draft, which in NBA terms means most teams had already looked at him and passed. Twenty-five players went before him. Twenty-five teams decided there was someone they wanted more than Mark Price. Those franchises have had nine years since then to reflect quietly on that decision.

Price became one of the greatest point guards of his era, a four-time All-Star who ran the Cavaliers offense with the kind of precision that made basketball look easy and made defenders look foolish. His shooting was extraordinary. In the 1993 NBA Three-Point Contest he shot 100 percent in one round, making all 25 attempts, a perfect score that has never been matched. That is not an impressive performance. That is a physics demonstration.

What made Price special beyond the shooting was his command of the game. He was not physically imposing, listed at six feet even, which in the NBA is the height equivalent of showing up to a skyscraper competition with a very nice two-story house, but he played bigger than his measurements in every way that mattered. Cleveland fans who grew up watching him understand exactly what they had, and they have never stopped being proud of it.

8. Brad Daugherty: The Big Man Cleveland Built Around (1986–1994)

When the Cavaliers selected Brad Daugherty with the first overall pick in the 1986 draft, they were not just adding a center. They were installing the anchor that everything else would be built around. Daugherty was seven feet tall, could score in the post, pass out of the double team, and anchor a defense in a way that gave Cleveland a genuine identity as a team that could compete with anyone in the Eastern Conference.

He made five All-Star teams in eight seasons, numbers that would place him among the most decorated big men of his generation if more people remembered to include him in that conversation. The Cavaliers teams of the late 1980s and early 1990s, the ones built around Daugherty and Price and Larry Nance, were legitimate contenders. They won consistently. They played beautiful, unselfish basketball. They were the kind of team that makes a city fall in love with the sport itself, not just the wins.

A knee injury ended his career far too early at just 28 years old, which is one of the genuinely cruel what-ifs in Cavaliers history. Daugherty never got to see how far that core group might have gone with him healthy. But in Cleveland he is remembered exactly as he should be, as one of the best big men this franchise has ever put on the floor, a player who made every teammate around him better and made Cavaliers basketball worth watching every single night.

9. LeBron James: The Kid from Akron Who Changed Everything (2003–2010, 2014–2018)

Thirty miles south of Cleveland sits the city of Akron, Ohio, and in the early 2000s a teenager was playing high school basketball there so spectacularly that national television networks were airing his games live. His name was LeBron James. By the time he graduated he was already being discussed as a potential generational talent, the kind of player who arrives once or twice in a lifetime and rearranges everything around them the way a really large piece of furniture rearranges an entire room.

The Cavaliers won the draft lottery in 2003 and selected LeBron first overall, and from his very first season he was everything the hype had promised and then a little more on top of that. He won Rookie of the Year, made the All-Star team, and within three years had carried a Cavaliers roster of supporting players who, on most other teams, would have been the fourth and fifth options all the way to the NBA Finals. In 2009 he was named league MVP. He was doing things on a basketball court that required new vocabulary to properly describe.

When he left for Miami in 2010 it hurt, badly and publicly, in a way that Cleveland sports fans felt in their chest. When he came back in 2014 and promised to bring a championship home, the city believed him because he had already shown them what he was capable of. What happened in 2016 is the subject of its own chapter, and it deserves every word it gets. LeBron James is the greatest player in Cavaliers history and one of the greatest to ever play the game. He is from thirty miles down the road. Cleveland gets to say that forever.

10. Kyrie Irving: The Most Unguardable Six Feet in Basketball (2011–2017)

Kyrie Irving handles a basketball the way a magician handles a deck of cards. Technically you can see exactly what his hands are doing and it somehow still makes no sense. Defenders who had studied him, prepared for him, and were actively trying to stop him would watch him change direction mid-dribble and end up facing completely the wrong way, as though the floor had quietly rotated underneath them while nobody was looking.

Cleveland drafted Kyrie first overall in 2011 and immediately had something the league had never quite seen before. He won Rookie of the Year, made six All-Star teams, and developed into one of the most creative offensive players of his generation. His ball-handling was not just a skill, it was a form of expression, a constant improvisation that made every possession feel like something surprising was about to happen. Fans bought tickets specifically to watch the moves he made between the dribbles.

The moment that defines his time in Cleveland is a pull-up three-pointer with 53 seconds left in Game 7 of the 2016 Finals, a shot that gave Cleveland the lead they never surrendered. He drilled it over the reigning MVP, in the biggest moment of the biggest game, without a trace of hesitation. More on that in Chapter 3. Just know that when you watch that shot and feel the arena explode, the man holding the ball had been dreaming about exactly that moment his whole life, and Cleveland was lucky enough to be the city he got to do it for.

11. The Decision

On July 8, 2010, LeBron James sat down in front of television cameras at a Boys and Girls Club in Greenwich, Connecticut, and participated in a one-hour ESPN special built entirely around announcing which basketball team he had decided to join. The special was called The Decision. It was, by any reasonable measure, a lot. Forty-five minutes of buildup, celebrity interviews, and careful misdirection before the actual answer arrived, and when it did, LeBron announced he was leaving Cleveland to join Dwyane Wade and Chris Bosh in Miami.

Cleveland responded the way you would expect a city to respond when the greatest player it had ever produced, a man who grew up thirty miles away and had once promised to bring a championship home, chose a beach city over them on national television. Fans burned jerseys in the street. Cavaliers owner Dan Gilbert published a furious open letter to fans that became famous partly for its content and partly because he wrote the whole thing in Comic Sans font, which is a creative choice that history has not been kind to. The letter promised Cleveland would win a championship before LeBron did, which turned out to be incorrect.

LeBron won two championships in Miami, in 2012 and 2013, and Cleveland watched both of them happen from a distance. It was a genuinely painful four years for the fan base. But the story was not over, and deep down most Cleveland fans probably knew it.

12. The Return

In August 2014, LeBron James published an essay announcing he was coming back to Cleveland, and the city's reaction made every jersey bonfire from 2010 feel like a distant memory. He was coming home. He was coming home specifically to try to win Cleveland the championship it had been waiting decades to celebrate. The whole city seemed to exhale at once.

What made the return meaningful beyond the basketball was what LeBron said about why he was doing it. He talked about Northeast Ohio, about the people who had shaped him, about owing something to the place he came from. He was not coming back because it was the easy path. The Warriors were already one of the best teams in the league. Miami had been a proven winner. Cleveland was a rebuild project that needed him to be everything, every single night. He chose it anyway.

The Cavaliers quickly added Kyrie Irving and Kevin Love to build a genuine contender around him, and within a year Cleveland was back in the NBA Finals. They lost that first series to Golden State in six games, which stung, but the message was clear. The Cavaliers were built for this. They would be back. And when they came back the following year, they came back with a story nobody in basketball history had ever managed to write before.

13. Down 3 to 1

The 2016 NBA Finals pitted the Cleveland Cavaliers against the Golden State Warriors, who had just finished the regular season with 73 wins, the best record in NBA history. The Warriors were the defending champions, loaded with talent, playing at home in Games 1, 2, 5, and 7, and widely considered one of the greatest teams ever assembled. Cleveland went down three games to one in the series, meaning Golden State needed just one more win across three remaining games to close it out.

At that point in NBA history, no team had ever come back from a 3-1 deficit in the Finals. Not one, in the entire history of the league. Every analyst, every statistical model, every reasonable observer looked at the situation and saw the same thing: this was over. The Warriors were too good, the math was too brutal, and Cleveland had simply run out of room.

The Cavaliers won Game 5 in Oakland. Then they won Game 6 in Cleveland. Then they flew back to Oakland for Game 7 and did something that had never been done before, which is the part of the story that still does not feel completely real no matter how many times you watch it happen.

14. The Block, The Shot, The Stop

Game 7 of the 2016 NBA Finals came down to the final two minutes with the score tied at 89, and in those two minutes the Cavaliers produced three separate moments that Cleveland fans will be describing to their grandchildren in considerable detail.

First came The Block. With about 1 minute 50 seconds remaining, Warriors guard Andre Iguodala had the ball in the open court and was heading toward what looked like a go-ahead layup. LeBron James, coming from the other end of the floor, tracked him down from behind and pinned the ball against the backboard. A chase-down block, in Game 7 of the Finals, with the season on the line, from a man who had started the play on the opposite end of the court. It is one of the most athletic plays in Finals history and it kept the score tied.

Then came The Shot. Kyrie Irving received the ball near the top of the key with 53 seconds left, dribbled left, and pulled up over Steph Curry for a three-pointer that dropped through the net and gave Cleveland a 92-89 lead. Pure, cold-blooded, no hesitation, over the reigning MVP of the league. The kind of shot that players practice imagining and rarely get the chance to actually take.

Then came The Stop. Golden State had chances to tie or take the lead in the final seconds and could not convert. The Cavaliers secured the rebound on the Warriors' last real possession, LeBron made two free throws to push the lead to four, and when the final buzzer sounded Cleveland had won 93-89. The city had its championship.

15. Fifty-Two Years

When the Cavaliers won the 2016 NBA Championship, they ended a drought that had been sitting on Cleveland sports like a very heavy piece of furniture nobody could figure out how to move. The last time a Cleveland team had won a major professional sports championship was 1964, when the Browns won the NFL title. That was 52 years. Two full generations of Cleveland fans had been born, grown up, and grown old without seeing their city win anything.

The Indians had not won a World Series since 1948. The Browns had not appeared in a Super Bowl in their entire existence. Cleveland had become so associated with near-misses and heartbreaks. Cleveland's heartbreaks practically had their own Wikipedia pages. The Drive. The Fumble. The Shot. Jose Mesa. Art Modell moving the Browns to Baltimore in the middle of the night. The list was long enough that out-of-town fans had started citing it the way people cite a menu, picking their favorite Cleveland tragedy to bring up at the worst possible moment.

LeBron James, a man from Akron who had promised to bring this city a championship and then spent four years in Miami before coming back to actually do it, fell to the floor in tears when the final buzzer sounded. The scenes in Cleveland that night were the kind you do not forget, people pouring into the streets, strangers hugging strangers, a city releasing 52 years of patience all at once. It was the loudest silence finally broken. Cleveland had waited long enough, and when it finally happened, it happened in the most dramatic way the sport has ever seen.

Cleveland fans pack the streets outside Quicken Loans Arena during the Cavaliers' 2016 championship parade. Wine-and-gold everywhere. After 52 years, the city finally celebrates a champion. *Photo: Cleveland Cavaliers Championship Parade (2016). Photograph by Erik Drost. Licensed under CC BY 2.0. Source: Wikimedia Commons.*

16. Rocket Mortgage FieldHouse: The Best Address in Cleveland

After years of packing fans into an arena surrounded by cornfields, Cleveland finally came back to the city itself in 1994 when the Cavaliers moved into a brand new downtown arena that would eventually become Rocket Arena, and the cows of Richfield Township have reportedly never fully recovered from the loss of the crowd noise.

Rocket Arena, known for most of its life as Rocket Mortgage FieldHouse, opened in 1994 under the considerably less corporate name of Gund Arena. Over the decades it has been renovated, renamed, and upgraded into one of the finest arenas in the NBA. A major transformation completed in 2019 added new clubs, wider concourses, better sightlines, and the kind of amenities that make you briefly forget you are supposed to be watching basketball because the food options are genuinely distracting. The building cost around $185 million to renovate, which is a lot of money to spend on a place where grown men throw a ball through a hoop, but nobody in Cleveland is complaining.

What makes the FieldHouse special is not the architecture. It is what happens inside it when the Cavaliers are good and the crowd is fully invested. The arena holds just over 19,000 fans, and when those 19,000 people decide to be loud, the building earns its reputation as one of the most hostile places in the league for visiting teams to play. The energy in 2016, during the championship run, reached levels that people in attendance still struggle to describe accurately without resorting to gestures.

The arena was renamed Rocket Arena in 2025, dropping the Mortgage from the title in a move that presumably made the signage slightly cheaper to print. The basketball inside remains the same quality regardless of what the building is called. This is the kind of thing that happens in modern professional sports and everyone quietly accepts because the basketball is still great and the renovation really was very good.

17. Moondog: The Mascot with the Most Committed Hair in Sports

The Cavaliers mascot is named Moondog, and he is a large, fuzzy, vaguely canine creature with an enormous shaggy blond mane that looks like he lost a bet with a lion and decided to just lean into it. Moondog has been the Cavaliers' official mascot for a number of years now, named after the famous Cleveland disc jockey Alan Freed, who popularized the term rock and roll in the 1950s and went by the nickname Moondog on the radio. It is a genuinely good backstory for a mascot, which puts Moondog ahead of about half the mascots in the league who are named after things like geographic features or weather patterns.

Moondog does the things all NBA mascots do: he fires t-shirts into the upper deck from a cannon, dances during timeouts, and interacts with fans in ways that are either charming or chaotic depending on your tolerance for large, costumed characters running at full speed in your direction. He has been ejected from a game at least once for arguing with a referee, which is honestly a level of commitment that deserves more recognition than it gets.

In a league full of mascots competing for attention, Moondog holds his own on personality alone. The hair helps.

18. The Wine and Gold: Why Cleveland's Colors Hit Different

There are teams in the NBA whose colors you could swap with another team and nobody would notice for a week. Cleveland is not one of those teams. The wine and gold combination is specific enough, warm enough, and distinct enough that it belongs to the Cavaliers the way a signature belongs to a person. You see those colors and you know exactly who you are looking at.

The identity runs deeper than the uniforms. Wine and gold shows up on the flags people hang outside their houses, the scarves wrapped around necks at games in January, the face paint choices of very committed fans who are having a significantly better time than the people sitting next to them. It is the kind of color scheme that requires no explanation within Northeast Ohio and requires about one second of explanation to anyone from anywhere else.

The brief period in the 1990s when the team wore dark navy and black gets brought up occasionally, usually as a cautionary tale about what happens when you let a focus group make aesthetic decisions. The wine and gold came back. It always comes back. Some things are just correct.

19. Cleveland's Sports Identity: A City That Shows Up

Cleveland is not a city that follows its teams when things are going well and finds something else to do when they are not. That is not how it works here. The Cavaliers have sold out games during rebuilding seasons, during losing streaks, and during stretches of the schedule where the most exciting thing happening on the court was a particularly competitive jump ball. Northeast Ohio shows up because showing up is what Northeast Ohio does, and if you need that explained then you probably did not grow up there.

The city itself shapes the fan base in ways that are hard to manufacture elsewhere. Cleveland is a working-class town, unpretentious and direct, the kind of place where people root for teams the same way they do everything else, with full commitment and no performance involved. There are no fair-weather Cavaliers fans in the sense that the weather in Cleveland between November and April does not particularly reward fairness from anyone. You bundle up, you drive in, and you cheer because the alternative is unthinkable.

What you get from that kind of culture is a fan base that genuinely means it. The noise in Rocket Arena during a playoff run is not manufactured enthusiasm. It is the sound of a city that has invested something real and wants something real back. Players who come to Cleveland and buy into that relationship tend to love it. The ones who do not tend to find out quickly that Cleveland fans can tell the difference, and they remember it either way.

20. Famous Cavs Fans and the City That Bleeds Wine and Gold

Cleveland has produced and claimed an impressive range of famous fans over the years. Drew Carey, the comedian and longtime host of The Price Is Right, is famously devoted to Cleveland sports and has been spotted at Cavaliers games more times than some of the players' own family members. Machine Gun Kelly, the musician, is a Cleveland native and a visible Cavs supporter. Gloria Estefan once performed at the arena, which is slightly different from being a fan but feels worth mentioning because it is a name nobody expected to appear in a basketball book.

Beyond the regulars, the Cavaliers have attracted some memorable courtside visitors over the years. During Game 3 of the 2016 Eastern Conference Finals against the Boston Celtics, with Cleveland dismantling the Celtics by 30 points, a familiar furry figure appeared in a courtside seat during the second half. Chewbacca, present as a promotional appearance for a new Star Wars film, sat ringside and watched the Cavaliers demolish Boston, which raises the question of whether the Wookie was good luck, bad luck for the Celtics, or simply a very large Star Wars fan with excellent taste in basketball teams.

The most genuinely touching courtside moment came in May 2024 when LeBron James, his Lakers eliminated from the playoffs, showed up at Rocket Arena to watch the Cavaliers face the Boston Celtics in the second round. The arena introduced him over the public address system as if he had never left, the crowd rose to give him a standing ovation, and LeBron responded by blowing kisses back into the stands. A man who had won championships in Miami and Los Angeles, sitting courtside in Cleveland, blowing kisses to the crowd that first believed in him. Some relationships just do not expire.

21. Donovan Mitchell Arrives: The Trade That Changed Everything

In September 2022, the Cleveland Cavaliers traded for Donovan Mitchell, the three-time All-Star guard from the Utah Jazz, and the basketball world took notice in a way it does not always take notice of Cleveland. The trade cost the Cavaliers three unprotected first-round picks and two pick swaps, which is a significant price by any measure, the kind of haul that makes other general managers either wince or immediately start calling to ask if there are any more of those available.

Mitchell is exactly the kind of player teams mortgage futures for. He can score from anywhere on the court, elevate in the biggest moments, and carry an offense through stretches when nothing else is working. He averaged over 28 points per game in his first full season in Cleveland, made the All-Star team, and immediately gave the Cavaliers the star-level scorer they had been missing since LeBron's departure. The city warmed to him quickly, which is the Cleveland way when a player shows up and immediately demonstrates he is there to work.

The Cavaliers had quietly built something serious before Mitchell even arrived, with young talent already in place that would have made Cleveland interesting without him. Adding Mitchell turned interesting into genuinely dangerous, and the rest of the league adjusted their opinion of Cleveland accordingly.

22. Evan Mobley: The Unicorn Cleveland Didn't Know It Needed

When the Cavaliers selected Evan Mobley with the third overall pick in the 2021 draft, they added a player so difficult to categorize that scouts spent the entire pre-draft process inventing new terms for what he was. Mobley stands seven feet tall, moves like a guard, passes like a point forward, and defends with the instincts of someone who has studied every opponent's tendencies since childhood and found them all somewhat predictable.

He was named to the All-Rookie team in his first season and finished second in Defensive Player of the Year voting in just his second year in the league, which is the kind of thing that usually takes a player five or six years to achieve and which Mobley accomplished while still being younger than most college seniors. His ability to protect the rim, switch onto guards on the perimeter, and initiate offense from the high post gives Cleveland a tactical flexibility that most teams would trade significant assets to have, which is somewhat ironic given that they already have him.

Mobley is the kind of player who makes coaching easier, which is the highest compliment you can pay a big man. You draw up a play, you put the ball in his hands, and more often than not something good happens. Cleveland found him with the third pick in a draft most people were not expecting to be particularly deep. That is either excellent scouting or excellent fortune, and the Cavaliers are wise enough not to spend too much time figuring out which one it was.

23. Darius Garland: The Point Guard Running the Show

Darius Garland was the fifth overall pick in the 2019 draft, which means he arrived in Cleveland two full years before the current core started coming together, making him the earliest piece of a puzzle that took a while to reveal its picture. His first two seasons were developmental, the kind of early chapters that look much more significant in hindsight once you can see where the story ends up.

By his third season, Garland had transformed into one of the better young point guards in the Eastern Conference, making his first All-Star appearance in 2022 and demonstrating the kind of playmaking vision that turns decent offenses into genuinely hard-to-guard ones. He sees passes before the defense does, operates at a pace that keeps opponents constantly adjusting, and has developed a mid-range game efficient enough to demand respect from defenders who would otherwise sag off him.

Playing alongside Donovan Mitchell since 2022 has accelerated everything. The two guards complement each other in ways that give opposing defenses genuine problems, with Garland's playmaking and Mitchell's scoring creating a combination that is difficult to plan for and even harder to stop in the moment. Cleveland fans who watched his early developmental seasons with patience have been rewarded with a player who looks exactly like what he was always supposed to become.

24. Jarrett Allen: The Quiet Anchor Nobody Talks About Enough

Every great team has a player who does not appear in enough highlight reels relative to how important he actually is, and for Cleveland that player is Jarrett Allen. The center is listed at six feet eleven inches, can run the floor like someone considerably shorter, and defends the paint with a consistency that does not generate viral moments so much as prevent the other team's viral moments from happening in the first place.

Allen was acquired from Brooklyn in the James Harden trade in 2021, arriving somewhat quietly and then proceeding to become one of the best defensive centers in the Eastern Conference. He has led the league in field goal percentage, which means that when Jarrett Allen attempts a shot he makes it at a rate that should make shooting coaches genuinely emotional. He does not force bad shots. He does not demand the ball in situations where someone else is better positioned. He does the things that win basketball games and does not appear to require constant recognition for doing them, which in the modern NBA is either extremely mature or extremely unusual, and possibly both.

On a roster with Mitchell, Mobley, and Garland each capable of lighting up a box score in very visible ways, Allen is the foundation underneath all of it. Teams trying to attack the Cleveland paint have to account for him on every possession. That kind of deterrence does not show up in the stat sheet as dramatically as it shows up in the outcome, and the outcome is what the Cavaliers are building toward.

25. Built to Last: Cleveland's Next Chapter

The Cleveland Cavaliers are one of the youngest serious contenders in the NBA, built around a core of players who have not yet reached the age at which most great players actually peak, which is either an exciting thought or a terrifying one depending on whether you are a Cavaliers fan or someone who has to play against them. Mobley, Garland, and Allen are all still in their early to mid twenties. Mitchell is in his prime. The foundation is deep, the roster is balanced, and the front office has demonstrated it is willing to make the kind of moves that turn contenders into champions.

Cleveland has been through enough as a sports city to know that nothing is guaranteed, that leads can disappear and injuries arrive without scheduling in advance and the difference between a dynasty and a near-miss can come down to a single bounce in a single game. They know this better than most. The history is right there in Chapter 1 if you need a reminder.

But this team is different from the ones that broke hearts in the past, and not just because of the talent level. It was built methodically, developed patiently, and reinforced at the right moments with the right players. It does not rely on one transcendent individual to carry every possession. It has multiple answers, multiple threats, and multiple reasons for opposing coaches to lose sleep.

Fifty-two years of waiting ended in 2016. The Cavaliers are not interested in waiting that long again, and based on what they have assembled, they should not have to.

Bonus Trivia Quiz!

You think you are a true Cavaliers fan? Try this bonus quiz!

1. Who won the fan naming contest that gave Cleveland its team name?

A) Nick Mileti
B) Jerry Tomko
C) Alan Freed
D) Dan Gilbert

2. What was the Cavaliers' win-loss record in their very first NBA season?

A) 23-59
B) 20-62
C) 15-67
D) 18-64

3. The Richfield Coliseum was unusual for an NBA arena because it was located where?

A) Inside a converted factory building
B) On the shores of Lake Erie
C) In a rural area surrounded by farmland between Cleveland and Akron
D) Underground, built into a hillside

4. What happened to center Jim Chones before the 1976 Eastern Conference Finals?

A) He was suspended for missing practice
B) He broke his foot in practice two days before the series
C) He tore his ACL in Game 4 against Washington
D) He was traded at the deadline

5. The NBA rule preventing teams from trading first-round picks in consecutive years was named after which Cavaliers owner?

A) Nick Mileti
B) Gordon Gund
C) Dan Gilbert
D) Ted Stepien

6. Austin Carr was selected by Cleveland with which draft pick in 1971?

A) Third overall
B) First overall
C) Fifth overall
D) Second overall

7. How many attempts did Mark Price make in his perfect round at the 1993 NBA Three-Point Contest?

A) 20

B) 30

C) 25

D) 15

8. Brad Daugherty was selected first overall in the 1986 draft and made how many All-Star teams during his career?

A) Three

B) Four

C) Six

D) Five

9. Where did LeBron James hold his 2010 announcement special known as The Decision?

A) Quicken Loans Arena in Cleveland

B) A Boys and Girls Club in Greenwich, Connecticut

C) American Airlines Arena in Miami

D) Madison Square Garden in New York

10. How many wins did the Golden State Warriors record in the regular season before the 2016 NBA Finals?

A) 67

B) 70

C) 73

D) 69

11. Whose layup did LeBron James block from behind in the final two minutes of Game 7 of the 2016 Finals?

A) Steph Curry

B) Klay Thompson

C) Draymond Green

D) Andre Iguodala

12. How many seconds were left on the clock when Kyrie Irving hit his famous three-pointer in Game 7?

A) 35 seconds

B) 53 seconds

C) 1 minute 10 seconds

D) 48 seconds

13. The last time a Cleveland team had won a major professional sports championship before 2016 was what year?

A) 1948
B) 1964
C) 1954
D) 1971

14. Cavaliers mascot Moondog was named after a Cleveland disc jockey who popularized what phrase?

A) Hip hop
B) Jazz music
C) Rock and roll
D) Soul music

15. Donovan Mitchell was traded to Cleveland from which team in September 2022?

A) Memphis Grizzlies
B) Dallas Mavericks
C) Utah Jazz
D) Denver Nuggets

Super Fan Secret Challenge

Only a true Cavaliers fan will know this.

(No Answer Provided)

In the 1976 playoff run known as the Miracle of Richfield, the Cavaliers defeated the defending NBA champion Washington Bullets in a thrilling Game 7. One Cavaliers player delivered a performance so memorable that Cleveland fans still talk about it today. Who was it?

A) Austin Carr
B) Jim Cleamons
C) Bingo Smith
D) Dick Snyder

Answer Key

1. B) Jerry Tomko

2. C) 15-67

3. C) In a rural area surrounded by farmland between Cleveland and Akron

4. B) He broke his foot in practice two days before the series

5. D) Ted Stepien

6. B) First overall

7. C) 25

8. D) Five

9. B) A Boys and Girls Club in Greenwich, Connecticut

10. C) 73

11. D) Andre Iguodala

12. B) 53 seconds

13. B) 1964

14. C) Rock and roll

15. C) Utah Jazz

NBA PLAYOFF BRACKET

First Round	Semifinals	Conf. Finals	Finals	Conf. Finals	Semifinals	First Round

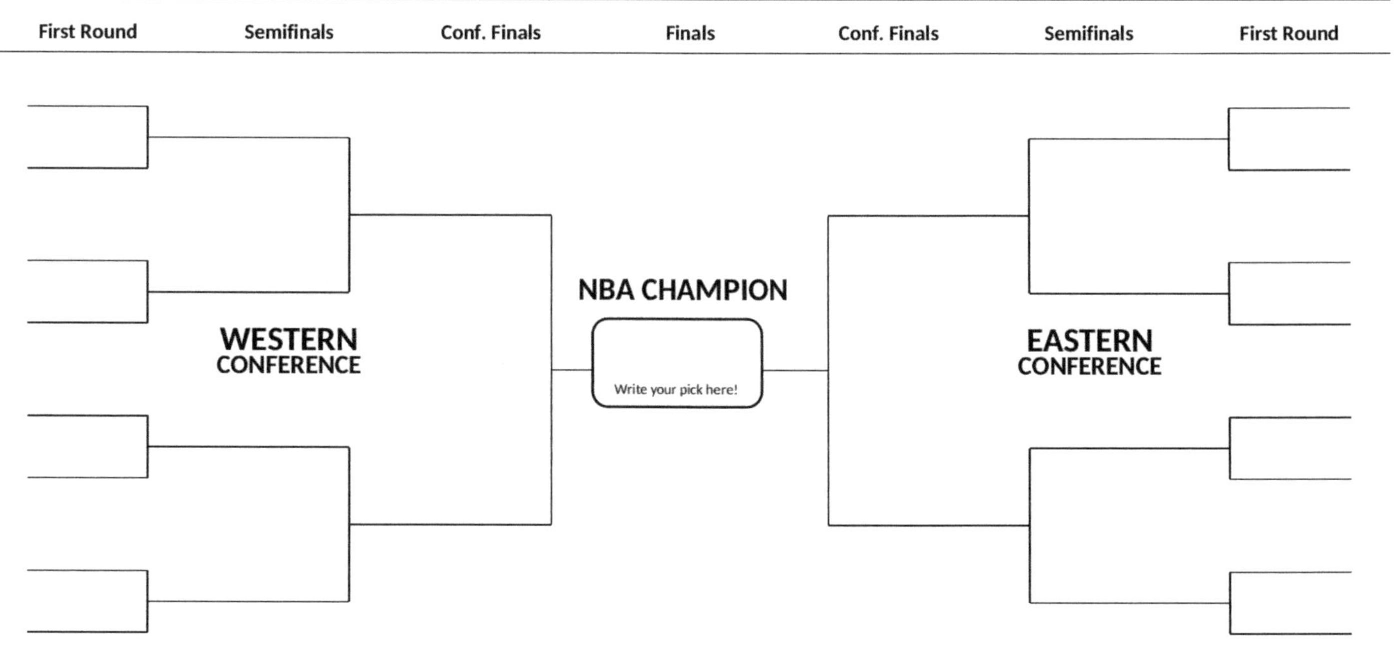

* Fill in your picks and try not to argue with your friends about it!

Part of the Fun Fan Facts: The Unofficial Sports Guide Series

Be the Boss of the Playoffs

You've broken down the matchups. You know which superstar takes over in the fourth quarter. You've seen the bench units that quietly decide series. You've watched the adjustments coaches make when their backs are against the wall.

Now it's time to stop watching and start deciding.

On this page, you are not just a fan. You are the Head Coach drawing up the last play with three seconds left on the clock. You are the GM who built this roster. You are the analyst who saw it all coming.

This is not just filling out a bracket.

This is building your championship run.

Sixteen teams enter the NBA Playoffs. The path is brutal. Best of seven. No shortcuts. No hiding. Every round gets louder, harder, and more personal.

This bracket is your Playoff Control Room.

The Game Plan

1. Survive Round One: Start with the opening round. Which matchup is going seven games? Who has the closer? Who folds under pressure? Make the calls.

2. Feel the Momentum: As you move into the Conference Semifinals and Conference Finals, things change. Role players become heroes. Stars feel the weight. Trust your reads.

3. Own the Finals: Trace your picks all the way to the NBA Finals. When the confetti falls and the trophy is raised, you'll find out who earned it.

House Rules: Circle your boldest upset. That is your official "I knew it" moment.

Choose Your Weapon: Pencil if you want flexibility. Pen if you trust your instincts. Sharpie if you believe in chaos.

Because once the playoffs tip off, there is no rewinding Game 7.

Make your picks. Trust your basketball brain. And let the playoff drama begin.

Fun Facts Wrap-Up

You made it through! You're officially a true superfan! Now it's time to put your knowledge to the test. Share these facts with friends and see who really knows their team best.

Love the series?

Your reviews help other fans discover Fun Fan Facts. If you enjoyed this book, we'd really appreciate you sharing your thoughts and leaving a review.

Want more Fun Fan Facts?

Scan the QR code below to visit our site and explore bonus trivia, challenges, and special extras - including new teams, future series, and collectible fun as they're released.

Collect All the Fun Fan Facts Series!

Check off every book you read. See the full set on Amazon. Search "Fun Fan Facts Jake Liam."

World Cup 2026 Edition

- ☐ Algeria
- ☐ Argentina
- ☐ Australia
- ☐ Austria
- ☐ Belgium
- ☐ Brazil
- ☐ Canada
- ☐ Cape Verde
- ☐ Colombia
- ☐ Croatia
- ☐ Curaçao
- ☐ Ecuador
- ☐ Egypt
- ☐ England
- ☐ France
- ☐ Germany
- ☐ Ghana
- ☐ Haiti
- ☐ Iran
- ☐ Ivory Coast
- ☐ Japan
- ☐ Jordan
- ☐ Mexico
- ☐ Morocco
- ☐ Netherlands
- ☐ New Zealand
- ☐ Norway
- ☐ Panama
- ☐ Paraguay
- ☐ Portugal
- ☐ Qatar
- ☐ Saudi Arabia
- ☐ Scotland
- ☐ Senegal
- ☐ South Africa
- ☐ South Korea
- ☐ Spain
- ☐ Switzerland
- ☐ Tunisia
- ☐ United States
- ☐ Uruguay
- ☐ Uzbekistan

World Cup 2026 Group Edition

- ☐ Group A
- ☐ Group B
- ☐ Group C
- ☐ Group D
- ☐ Group E
- ☐ Group F
- ☐ Group G
- ☐ Group H
- ☐ Group I
- ☐ Group J
- ☐ Group K
- ☐ Group L

English Football Edition

☐ Arsenal F.C.

☐ Aston Villa F.C.

☐ Chelsea F.C.

☐ Everton F.C.

☐ Fulham F.C.

☐ Liverpool F.C.

☐ Manchester City

☐ Manchester United

☐ Newcastle United F.C.

☐ Tottenham Hotspur

☐ West Ham United

☐ Wrexham A.F.C.

NBA Edition

☐ Atlanta Hawks

☐ Boston Celtics

☐ Brooklyn Nets

☐ Charlotte Hornets

☐ Chicago Bulls

☐ Cleveland Cavaliers

☐ Dallas Mavericks

☐ Denver Nuggets

☐ Detroit Pistons

☐ Golden State Warriors

☐ Houston Rockets

☐ Indiana Pacers

☐ LA Clippers

☐ Los Angeles Lakers

☐ Memphis Grizzlies

☐ Miami Heat

☐ Milwaukee Bucks

☐ Minnesota Timberwolves

☐ New Orleans Pelicans

☐ New York Knicks

☐ Oklahoma City Thunder

☐ Orlando Magic

☐ Philadelphia 76ers

☐ Phoenix Suns

☐ Portland Trail Blazers

☐ Sacramento Kings

☐ San Antonio Spurs

☐ Toronto Raptors

☐ Utah Jazz

☐ Washington Wizards

About the Author

Jake is a 13-year-old sports fan who loves football, American football, and basketball. He plays soccer as a goalie and dreams of one day playing for West Ham United and helping teach kids to love the game. His passion for sports runs in the family - his dad was a professional baseball player, and his stepdad sparked his love for West Ham. Through the Fun Fan Facts series, he shares the fun and excitement of sports with fans everywhere.

www.ingramcontent.com/pod-product-compliance
Lightning Source LLC
Chambersburg PA
CBHW050040040726
47599CB00015B/1773